101 SURVIVAL TIPS

FOR

MISSIONARY MOMS

by

MARY YOACHUM

Illustrated by

Cherie Cox Johnson

The ideas and suggestions in this book are intended to help you make your experience as a missionary mom a happy and rewarding one. This book is written for the purpose of helping you to keep busy and to help you "survive" while your missionary is away. It is by no means a total list of everything you can do, but it is a start. These ideas will keep you busy and engaged in rewarding activities and will make you feel better emotionally and spiritually. Keeping busy will also make you feel that you are involved and are making a worthwhile contribution. It will enable you to feel that you are doing all you can to help and support your missionary while at the same time you are helping yourself. It will make you feel that you are a part of his mission. Remember if your missionary is happy, then you will be happy, and that's the key!

Although the ideas listed refer specifically to elders, they are also intended to be used for sister missionaries as well.

DEDICATED

TO

MY THREE SONS

PAUL--serving in the Germany Dusseldorf Mission. . .

BRIAN--serving in the Switzerland Zurich Mission. . .

ROBBIE--patiently waiting in the wings. . .

SAY "CHEESE"

Take a wide variety of pictures of your missionary before he leaves, including some in missionary clothes. After he is gone, display some of the pictures throughout the house; save the others to use in his scrapbook. Place the pictures in areas of your home where you can see them every day. Be certain to hang at least one or two on the refrigerator door. While your home may seem empty without him, looking at his pictures each day will help you feel a little closer to your son.

Suggested Ideas: Receiving his call
Going shopping
Receiving his patriarchal blessing
Going to the temple
Following his farewell
Getting set apart
Packing
Saying good-bye
Arriving at the MTC
Saying good-bye at the airport

MISSION MEMORIES

As soon as your son receives his call, begin to make a scrapbook. You may purchase a missionary scrapbook from a local bookstore, or make one to fit your own needs. You may want to divide it into sections; for example, **the call, the preparation, the farewell, the MTC, the airport, and the mission field,** including each area in which he serves. Include all his mission papers, pictures, cards, special correspondence, memorabilia, stamps, receipts, tickets, brochures, transfer papers, etc. There will be more than enough material to fill a book. Be certain to begin your scrapbook before your son is gone so that he can help with the planning. It will also help him to remember to send home important items to be included in his book.

LETTER FILE

Save all your son's letters. Do not try to put them in the scrapbook, but buy a separate folder or loose-leaf binder for them. You may wish to purchase a large quantity of clear plastic loose-leaf envelopes in which to store and protect the letters. Arrange the letters in chronological order beginning with the MTC. (Date the letters as you receive them). If you prefer you may purchase a large quantity of stationery which your son can take with him. He can use this for all his letters so that all the stationery you put in the loose leaf will be the same size. (On special occasions he may write letters on other things besides the regular stationery--menus or place mats, for example). But generally most of his letters will be written on the paper he has with him. Make certain that he always has an adequate supply, and have him notify you when he runs low so you can replenish his supply. Before you know it, the letters will begin to add up. Read these letters often, and you will be able to see the progress your son is making. Reading his letters will also bring you closer to your son, and he won't seem so far away.

VOICE MAIL

Buy two mini-cassette recorders/players, one for you and one for your son. Make tapes every month or two and send to your son. Have him do the same thing for you when he has the time. It's the next best thing to talking on the phone. Listening to his voice will help you, and you can be sure it will help him. Try to get the entire family and also some of his close friends to talk. Fill your missionary in on all the current news concerning your family and his friends. Tell him the things that are too lengthy to be written in a letter. Be sure that part of the tape includes your testimony and your joy and happiness in what he is doing. You can listen to the tapes over and over again.

COMPANION CONNECTION

If possible, find out where your son's companion's parents live and contact them by letter (or telephone if they are close by). It will help you to talk to another missionary mother, particularly one whose child is serving with your son and living with him 24 hours a day. Share and compare their experiences. Be sure to let your son know you have made contact with his companion's parents. This just may be the start of a special friendship.

COMMON BOND

Find out if there are other missionaries in your city or area who are currently serving in your son's mission. Make contact with their parents and share experiences, pictures, success stories, etc. It is very rewarding to bond with other missionary parents, particularly those whose children are in the same country, city, area, etc. as your son. In most cases the work and the missionary efforts will be nearly identical. Their concerns are your concerns, and you can build up and support one another. Your sons will no doubt face similar circumstances and challenges. More than likely, your sons are doing the same things.

CULTURE CLUB

Find out all you can about the country, state, city, area where your son is serving. Visit a local public library and get books, maps, pictures, videos, etc. Learn about the history, culture, customs, and language, so you will be more familiar with the place where your son will be spending two years of his life. It will make him seem nearer to you if you familiarize yourself with his country. No matter how far away he is, knowing something about his area will bring him closer. It will also help you to feel a bond to those people in that country who are members of the church.

NEWS AND NOTES

Send copies of your monthly ward newsletter to your missionary. This will enable him to be aware of what is happening in his ward and will keep him up to date on ward activities. If the ward or branch where your son is serving has a newsletter, ask your son to send some home with his letters.

This will enable you to see what is happening in his ward in another part of the world. Also send a current ward directory to your son so he will have access to names and addresses of ward members he may want to write.

THANK YOU!

Ask your son to send you the name and address (and a little background, if possible) of a special member family who has been kind, helpful, and generous to your son. Write to this family and thank them for supporting and helping your son and for making him feel welcome in their home. Express your appreciation for their kindness and concern.

CONFERENCE UPDATES

If your son is in an area where he cannot see or hear General Conference, record conference talks on cassette and send to him. He can listen to the tapes anytime and the talks might be helpful when he is looking for inspirational material and/or preparing a talk of his own.

INFORMATION, PLEASE!

Write to the country, state, city, or county chamber of commerce or government and ask them to send you brochures, pamphlets, maps, or any other information they may have about the area where your son is serving.

BON VOYAGE

Visit a local travel agency or bureau in your city. Obtain brochures about the foreign country or state where your son is serving.

REMEMBER WHEN?

Try to locate someone in your area who has returned from the same mission where your son is. Visit him or invite him to your home for a family home evening or dinner. Ask him to bring his scrapbook or special pictures, and ask him to share his experiences with you. Take his picture with your family, and send it to your son along with a letter about your evening together.

SPECIAL SPOTLIGHT

Arrange with your bishop to do a spotlight every three or four months on the missionaries in your ward. Make a display on a ward bulletin board with pictures, letters, the missionary's testimony, etc. This will let all ward members actually see what

15

the missionaries in your ward are doing and will help remind them about the importance of missionary work.

I HOPE THEY CALL ME ON A MISSION

Get everyone in your ward involved in the missionary program. Encourage the Young Women, Young Men, and Primary to help the missionaries by writing letters, making inexpensive gift boxes, drawing or taking pictures, writing personal testimonies, etc. The Primary children could even make a tape to send singing favorite Primary songs. A Primary sharing time could also be centered around the missionary program and the missionaries in your ward. This will help the Primary children become more familiar with the young men and women who are all over the world. If possible, have pictures of each missionary available, as well.

STORIES OF STRENGTH

Make copies of General Authorities' talks or articles from the **Ensign** or **New Era**, particularly inspirational and/or uplifting articles on missionary work, and send these to your son.

AS TIME GOES BY

Make or purchase a missionary time chart or missionary countdown calendar while your son is gone. In addition to counting off the days, record the dates of all transfers, baptisms, new companions, church callings, promotions, special experiences, faith-promoting stories, etc. Get brothers and sisters involved as well. Let each child have his own chart or calendar to count off the days and keep track of the time.

THINKING OF YOU

In addition to your own son, write letters, and send birthday and holiday cards to other missionaries in your ward and/or close friends of your son. Share some of your son's experiences with them and also build these missionaries up by letting them know what a great job they are doing. Let them know you are praying for them and thinking of them often.

KEEP IN TOUCH

Send pictures often of family and friends, and also new buildings, stores, homes, churches, etc. that have been built while your son is away. If you live in an area where there are four distinct seasons, take four pictures of your family outside in front of a tree, garden, or area that will clearly show each season. Remember that just as seasons change, so does your family. Younger brothers and sisters will change dramatically in the two years your son is gone. Let him see these changes.

CHOOSE THE RIGHT

If your son doesn't have one already, purchase a CTR ring (in foreign letters, if applicable) and send it to him for a special occasion.

SHARE THE MESSAGE

Send copies of a family group picture along with your personal testimony to your son to give to investigators with their copy of the **Book of Mormon**.

KEEPING SCORE

Clip and send news and magazine articles and current events which might be interesting to your missionary. These might be articles on sports, local school activities, programs, or events in your area.

PIN UPS

Purchase inexpensive LDS tie tacks, lapel pins, or CTR rings and send them to your son to give to newly baptized members.

STICK 'EM UP

Be sure to send holiday and LDS stickers to your son for him to use on his mail.

LETTERHEAD LUXURY

If you desire, purchase stationery with the name of your son's mission printed on it, and send it to him to use when he writes friends or family members.

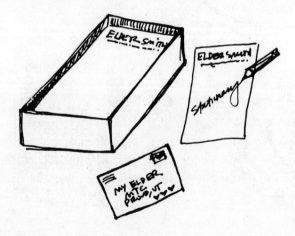

BE PREPARED

Always carry copies of your son's current address with you in your purse or wallet. You never know when you may "run into" someone who would like to write to your son. A good idea is to type the address on a sheet of mailing labels which can be easily and instantly applied to an envelope.

HELLO AND GOODBYE

Whenever possible, attend the farewells or homecomings of missionaries who will serve or have served in the same mission as your son. If the missionary is departing, give him your son's name and address; if he is returning, find out if he knows your son.

HISTORY AT A GLANCE

Make a current events scrapbook for your son while he is gone Include magazine and newspaper articles and pictures of important events which occurred in your neighborhood, city, state, country, etc. Make it quite general but compete enough so that he will be able to see what important events occurred during the two years he was away.

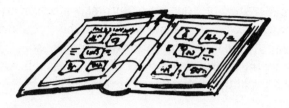

PRIESTHOOD POWER

After your son has left for his mission, get a priesthood blessing to comfort you and help you to be strong.

FAMILY MATTERS

In addition to your son's missionary scrapbook, make your own family scrapbook while your son is away. Include all the important things you do as a family including family activities, reunions, vacations, special occasions, etc.

DAILY DATA

Keep a daily journal. It helps to express your feelings in writing. Also you need to keep a daily record of your activities so you can always let your son know what things happened while he was gone.

KEEPING TRACK

Make a simple chart or list of all the letters/packages you send to your son. It will be helpful to you to see just how much you have written and reassure you that you are keeping him well supplied with cards and letters. Make a similar chart for all the cards, letters and packages you receive from him.

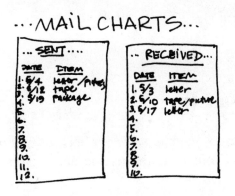

WRITE ON AND ON. . .

Be sure to write regularly. Include more than news and activities from home. Make your letters positive, encouraging, and uplifting. Constantly tell your son of your love for him and of your total support for what he is doing. Keep in mind that your son will have days of homesickness, discouragement, and disappointment, so bear your testimony to him often and let him know how much his mission is blessing your life. Let him know that the family is closer together and closer to the Lord because of his mission, his service, and his sacrifice. If you know that he is happy, then you will be happy yourself.

DEAR PRESIDENT:

Every four to six months write the mission president and his wife. Express your love, thanks and appreciation to them for their efforts and for their continued support, encouragement, and concern for your son.

GIVE GENEROUSLY

If your finances permit, give a little extra to your ward or stake missionary fund each month or every few months.

HOOKED ON CLASSICS

Find out from your son what type of music is allowed in his mission. Then buy some approved classical or church tapes, (buy two copies of each tape, so you will have some for yourself), and send the tapes to your son. He can listen to this music while he is studying or relaxing. You can likewise listen to the music while you are reading the scriptures. Find out what his favorites are and make them your favorites, too. As you listen, you will discover a real spiritual bond with your son.

WEEKDAY FAST

Fast on a day other than Fast Sunday. Base your fast on the success of the missionary program, both for your son and for the missionaries in your ward and stake.

BOOKS OF KNOWLEDGE

In addition to reading the scriptures, read and study the books your son reads--**Jesus the Christ, A Marvelous Work and a Wonder, Gospel Principles, Truth Restored.** Let your son know that you are reading these books. It will help him realize that you are committed to him and his mission and at the same time will increase your knowledge, faith, testimony, and spirituality. You will feel a real sense of accomplishment when you have completed this reading assignment. Encourage others to read these books also.

THE "WRITE" IDEA

Use variety in your letter writing. Every so often make up your own stationery or write letters on things other than standard paper. There are books available containing numerous ideas on how to do this.

KNOW YOUR RELIGION

Read and study the scriptures daily without fail--no matter how busy you might be. Set a time aside each day to do this when you know that you will not be interrupted.

"CALLING HOME"

Pray continually, not just in the morning and evening, but throughout the day. Ask for blessings for your son and the work he is doing. Ask for blessings for yourself and your family to enable you to handle the void left by your son's absence. Seek the Lord and ask for His spirit to abide with you at all times.

WE'VE BEEN THERE

Find out if there is a family in your area who is native to the country or state where your son is serving. Contact them and ask them to share some of their experiences with you. Take a picture of the family and send it to your son with information about these people.

YOU'RE INVITED!

Organize a ward or stake activity with other missionary families. This might be a dinner, a picnic, a talent show, or a program with a missionary theme. Share food, culture, language, customs, etc.

FLIGHT 525

While your son is in the MTC, contact his companion's parents. Arrange to meet them at the airport on the day of your son's departure. After your sons have gone, plan to keep in touch with each other through letters (or phone calls) and let each other know of your son's progress in the field.

IN THE HOUSE OF THE LORD

Go to the temple often. You will not only feel the spirit of the Lord but also the spirit of your son, and frequent temple attendance will keep you closer to the Lord. As you utter your silent prayers within the temple, you will feel reassurance from the Lord which will help to sustain you in your son's absence.

PARTY ON!

Just before your son leaves the MTC, send him and his companion a small box with party hats, balloons, noise makers, and confetti for a small going away party. It will help him celebrate and feel the excitement of a new beginning in his life.

BECOMING A SPIRITUAL GIANT

After your son has been in the mission field for six months, ask him to write his testimony and send it to you or the bishop. Have it read in a Sacrament Meeting or printed in a ward newsletter. His testimony will help increase your own testimony and testimonies of ward members as well. His testimony will build you up when you recognize how he has grown and matured spiritually.

FOR YOUR INFORMATION

When you or a member of your family gives a talk in church, make a copy and send it to your son. Perhaps the talk may be useful to him in some way when he has to prepare a talk or a lesson. When you have a special speaker in your ward for Sacrament Meeting or a fireside, record the talk on cassette (with the speaker's permission) and send it to your son.

DEPARTURE DATES

Send missionary farewell announcements and pictures from the newspaper of friends and acquaintances who are departing or returning from missions.

QUIPS AND QUOTES

Send your son a book of inspirational thoughts and quotes from general authorities or church leaders. They will be invaluable to him when he needs a quote for a talk or a presentation.

GIFT WRAP

Be sure to decorate your son's mail. On the outside of envelopes and packages, use stickers, notes, quotes, etc. to brighten up his mail.

MAGNETIC MEMORIZATION

Purchase two identical magnets with an inspirational thought or message on them. Send one to your son and keep one for yourself. Then twice a month, send your son one of your favorite scriptures for him to post with his magnet. Post the same scripture on your refrigerator. Choose scriptures which will be uplifting and useful to your son. Memorize each of the scriptures you send, and in two years you will have learned 48 scriptures.

PEN PALS

Have a brother or sister begin correspondence with a pen pal in the country or state where your son is serving. In addition to their letters, have them exchange pictures and postcards, and share school experiences, family activities, traditions, customs, etc.

MAY I TAKE YOUR ORDER?

When your family goes out to eat together, write your son a letter on a place mat or menu while you are at the restaurant. Have each member of the family write something, and let your son know that even though you're enjoying your outing, he is always in your thoughts no matter where you are or what you are doing. Receiving this letter will let him know that he is still an important and essential part of the family.

DO UNTO OTHERS

A good part of your son's mission involves service to others. At least once a week, do a service for someone in your ward or neighborhood (include inactive or non members as well). Make a loaf of bread, some cookies, offer to baby-sit, run an errand, help with household chores, gardening, etc. After a while, you will look forward to your weekly service projects, and more importantly, you will have a good feeling about what you are doing. You will be blessed for your efforts!

A FAMILY AFFAIR

Although you and/or your husband will be most actively involved in your son's mission, encourage all family members to become involved. In addition to weekly letters, have brothers and sisters draw pictures, write poems or stories, bear testimonies, or share faith-promoting experiences and send to your son.

TICKLE HIS FUNNY BONE

When you come across missionary cartoons in books or magazines, cut them out or copy them and send them to your son. He needs and will appreciate a little bit of humor now and then.

MISSIONARY MOM

At least one day a week, make an effort to devote an hour or two doing something related to missionary work.

HERE COMES THE BRIDE

Be sure to keep your missionary up to date on family and friends' activities at home including weddings, births, awards and recognitions received, outstanding achievements, new jobs, etc.

MEETING OF THE MINDS

Form a mothers' group with the mothers in your ward or neighborhood and meet once every month or two at a home, or if your prefer, at a restaurant for lunch. Compare notes, and share your sons' experiences with each other. As you discuss your concerns, you will realize that you all share a common bond.

TESTIMONY TIME

Bear your testimony often in church. Bear witness to the grand and glorious purpose of missionary work, and encourage all members to get involved.

WITNESS OF THE SPIRIT

Share uplifting and inspirational stories and experiences of your son with your friends and ward members.

HOLIDAY CHEER

Purchase or borrow a book of ideas on things to make and send your missionary on holidays, birthdays, and special occasions. There are numerous publications available. These books will help you to send a variety of fun and worthwhile things to your son. The books may also spark your imagination and enable you to make up ideas of your own. There is no limit to the things you can do.

FIDO AND FLUFFY

If you have family pets, don't forget to take their pictures, too, and send them to your son.

MAD MONEY

If you can do so safely, send your son a little extra money every so often so he can "splurge" and eat out once in a while or buy something that he would really like to have.

MOTHER'S DAY GIFT

Your missionary usually sends you a card and/or calls you on Mother's Day. He does something for you to honor you as his mother. To be different, send him a card or a special letter just prior to Mother's Day. Let him know how proud you are to be his mother and that your Mother's Day is special because of him. Tell him how he has blessed your life and how thankful you are to be his mother. Tell him that you must be the luckiest mother in the world because you have the best son in the world!

PUTTING IT TOGETHER

If possible, purchase a jigsaw puzzle of the country, state, area of the world where your son is serving. As you put the puzzle together with the family, take a picture of everyone working on it. When it is finished, take another picture of the completed puzzle and send it to your son.

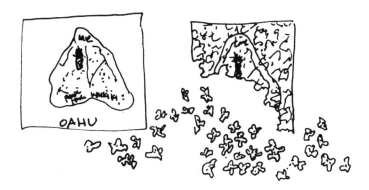

ONE FOR YOU AND ONE FOR ME

Whenever possible, when you send something to your son, send something for his companion as well (candy, cookies, stickers, etc).

JUST FOR FUN

Just for fun, make up your own holiday or special occasion to celebrate with your missionary. Buy or make a funny, inexpensive gift or card and send it to him with an explanation of what you are doing. He will love it, and will welcome a little bit of humor.

SO LONG, FAREWELL. . .

If possible, take a video camera to the airport. Record your son greeting and saying good-bye to family and friends and boarding the airplane. Replay this departure often while your son is gone. It may bring back a flood of tears, but how thankful you will be that you have this special occasion recorded. Use the same tape to record his arrival home and the joy that is there as he steps off the plane.

TIME MARCHES ON

If your son is in another time zone, set at least one clock in your house to the time it is in his area. If he is several hours ahead or behind, doing this will enable you to know immediately what time of day or night it is without having to stop and count hours.

A HOME AWAY FROM HOME

Take a real interest in the missionaries in your area. Get to know them and offer to help them whenever possible. Take them to the store, to run errands, to do their laundry, etc. Invite them to dinner, and let them know that they are always welcome in your home. Do little acts of kindness for them. Bake them some cookies, and make or buy small, inexpensive gifts for them on holidays. Find out when their birthday is and send them a card. You always hope that members of the church in another part of the world will be kind and helpful to your son, so make the effort to take care of someone else's son.

PLEASE COME

Make certain that you extend an invitation for dinner to the missionaries in your area on special holiday occasions like Christmas, Thanksgiving, Easter, etc. It will help them feel a little closer to home to be with a family on holidays.

LIVE FROM TEMPLE SQUARE

Invite the local missionaries to your home to watch or listen to a session of General Conference with your family. Prepare breakfast or lunch for them before or after the conference session.

MOM WILL BE PROUD

Take pictures of the missionaries in your area when they are in your home for lunch or dinner. Get their home addresses and then send these pictures to their parents with a note telling them how well their son is doing and how much you enjoy having him in your home

HELP US OUT!

Help the missionaries in your area by making referrals, and by giving them names of possible contacts. Visit nonmember or inactive neighbors and encourage them to let the missionaries come to visit. Be sure to follow through and contact the missionaries if these people agree.

A NEW MEMBER

If the missionaries in your area baptize someone you know well, make every effort to attend the baptism. It will not only show the new member that you care, but it will help you to draw closer to your own son by witnessing the baptism and remembering that this is what he is doing in another part of the world.

FUTURE MISSIONARY

If you have a son who is close to missionary age, encourage him to team up with the local missionaries every few months. It will be an excellent opportunity for him to see what missionary work is like, and it also helps the missionaries.

WHERE IN THE WORLD ARE YOU?

Be sure to obtain and display a detailed map of the area where your son is serving. Mark cities and towns as he is transferred.

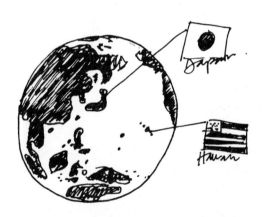

LIGHTS, CAMERA, ACTION

Make some videos for your son to watch when he comes back home. Record special occasions like birthday parties, family parties, holiday gatherings, school assemblies or activities, sporting events where family members are involved, graduations, wedding receptions, new babies, etc. Make another video of special programs on television, church programs and firesides, excerpts from major sporting events, world or national news milestones or events. Make certain that the programs you record are of value and importance. You can't record everything, and you need to be selective. But in two years' time you should have no trouble filling up two or three video tapes. It will mean a great deal to your son and will enable him to see the things that happened while he was gone.

VITAL STATISTICS

Be sure to keep track of church news, and send your son news of world-wide church activities and growth. Send articles about new temples or newly opened missions, new church leaders, world-wide membership, deaths of general authorities, etc. Also include new callings and releases in your ward and stake.

CONGRATULATIONS!

When your son has a baptism, receives a transfer, gets a new companion, is made a district or zone leader, a trainer, or an
52

AP, be sure to send a special letter or card expressing your joy at his progress.

POST IT

If it is possible and not too expensive, ask your son to send you a different postcard once a month. Save these and just before he returns home, make a collage of all the cards from that state or country.

ON THIS DATE. . .

At the end of each month, review your personal journal. Make a monthly calendar or a chronological list of important events, activities, special occasions, etc. which occurred during the preceding month. Then send this list to your son. Be brief, but thorough. This will enable him to see what his family has done or accomplished during the last 30 days. (Choose at least 10 items, but not more than 20).

DID WE SAY THAT?

Be sure to make a cassette tape of your son's farewell. When you need a lift, listen to the tape, and all the memories of that special day will return.

FAMILY, FRIENDS, AND FUN

If you have an open house or dinner following your son's farewell, have a friend or relative take pictures with a video camera. Also take plenty of snapshots of family members and friends as well.

ONE MORE ON HIS WAY

When you attend the farewell of a close friend of your son's, take a picture of him with members of your own family and send it to your son. Be sure to make an extra print for the missionary's parents as well.

YOU CAN DO IT!

Set a personal goal to accomplish something worthwhile while your son is gone. Develop a new talent, learn a new skill, start an exercise program, or anything else you want to do to improve yourself. Once you start something, stick to it every day, and be determined to achieve your goal. Have faith in yourself. Use your son's mission as an example, inspiration, and motivation to keep yourself going. Remember, if your son can do what he is doing, then so can you.

HELLO!

Most missionaries are allowed to call home twice a year--on Christmas and Mother's Day. If it is possible, make arrangements with your son to call him, particularly if he is in a foreign mission, because it will be less expensive. If you check the rates and call when they're lower, you can talk longer. Also plan ahead just what you want to say to him and ask him. Make a list because inevitably you cannot think of everything once you're on the phone. Arrange to have a speaker phone so everyone can hear him at the same time, and so more of you can talk to him in a shorter amount of time.

LEARN PATIENCE, MOM

On a day when you are anxiously awaiting a letter and one does not come, you will feel frustrated, discouraged, and perhaps even a little worried. But "hang in" there; the letter will come eventually. Rather than feeling down for the rest of the day, get your son's book of letters out and reread the last few. Surprisingly, it will cheer you up and make those "blues" go away.

WHAT DO YOU NEED?

Sometimes a missionary is in an area where it may be difficult
for him to obtain certain items, no matter how common they
may be. If this is the case, make up and send him a checklist
which he can mark indicating the items that he may need you to
send to him. This would be primarily food items, toiletries,
clothing, film, batteries, etc.

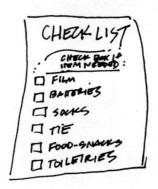

FOREIGN SCRIPTURE STUDY

If your son is in a foreign language mission, purchase a copy of
the **Book of Mormon** in that language. Although you may not
be able to read it, you can use it when you want to send special
scriptures to your son. Locate the scripture in your own **Book
of Mormon**, then find the corresponding scripture in the
foreign book. Copy it as it appears and send it to your son.
Although you cannot understand the scripture, your son will,

and this will in a small way help him with his scripture study.
Do this every few weeks.

BON APPETITE

Find out what foods are eaten in the country where your son is
serving. Every month or two prepare a dinner for your own
family similar to one that your son might be eating. This will
not only familiarize you with the food your son eats, but will
enable you to try new foods and see what people from other
cultures eat. Let your son know of your interest in the new
foods and ask him to send you recipes every now and then,
especially when he tries a new dish.

NAME THAT TUNE

If possible, purchase a hymn book in the language of the country where your son is serving. Learn to sing a hymn or two in that language and then record your song on a cassette, and send it to him. It will brighten his day to hear his family singing when he realizes that you have made the effort to do this for him. It will also make you feel good, too, and proud of yourself for what you have accomplished.

WELCOME, NEW MEMBERS

Get the name and address (and a little background information) of an individual or family recently baptized by your son. Write the new members a letter expressing your joy and happiness for them. Tell them how much your son loves them. If possible send the new members a picture of your family along with your testimony.

LICK 'EM AND STICK 'EM

If your son is serving in a foreign country, save all the different stamps from his letters. Mount them or make a collage and add this to his scrapbook.

DEUTSCHE, ANYONE?

Enroll in a foreign language class in a community education program. Or if you want college credit, sign up for a foreign language course. In one quarter you will learn enough so that you can write short, simple messages to your son in the language he is learning. He will be impressed!

"MOVING" MOVIES

Purchase a variety of church videos from the Distribution Center or an LDS bookstore. Watch these videos with your family while your son is gone. Many times missionaries have the opportunity to watch these same videos in the mission field. As you watch, you will be "moved" and will definitely feel the spirit of missionary work. Your son's mission will take on new meaning for you.

CAN YOU READ THIS?

Find a friend, relative, neighbor, or teacher who speaks the language of the country where your son is serving. Ask him to write a short letter to your missionary in that language. When your son receives it, he will have to use his foreign language skills to read it. It will be a positive experience for him because he will realize that he learning the language and making real progress.

LANGUAGE LESSON

If your son is in a country where a foreign language is spoken, ask him to write little messages at the end of his letters in that language. Purchase a foreign language dictionary at a bookstore; then figure out what the message says. When you write back, let your son know you have figured out the message by writing a reply or an answer to it in that language. It will make you feel that you've accomplished something and will also let your son know you are making the extra effort to learn a little about his language. Once you are a bit familiar with the language your son is learning, take the initiative and write your own short message to your son. If will be fun for him to figure it out and reply, as well.

ICH LIEBE DICH!
I LOVE YOU!
¡TE QUERO A TI!

WELCOME, HOME!

Near the end of his mission, make a coupon book for your son and send it to him. Offer coupons for fun activities with family and friends upon his arrival home. (Often, local restaurants will provide coupons or discounts for a meal to a returning missionary).